Feral Kingdom

Poems by James H. Duncan

Kung Fu Treachery Press
Rancho Cucamonga, CA

Copyright ©James H. Duncan, 2019
First Edition 1 3 5 7 9 10 8 6 4 2
ISBN: 978-1-950380-18-3
LCCN: 2019937359

Design, edits and layout: John T. Keehan, Jr.
Title page image: Jon Lee Grafton
Author photo: James H. Duncan
All rights reserved. No part of this publication may be reproduced or transmitted in any form or by any means, electronic or mechanical, including photocopying, recording or by info retrieval system, without prior written permission from the author.

Acknowledgements

I'd like to thank everyone who ever put me up, let me crash, bought me a drink, a meal, a ticket, a ride, and anyone who gave me a chance. I'd also like to thank all of the journals and magazines who published some of the poems within this collection, places like *The Blue Hour Review, Punch Drunk Press, Foliate Oak Literary Magazine, Picaroon Poetry, Up The River, Marble Poetry Magazine,* and *Epic Rites Press.*

This one is for my dad, JT.

-JHD

CONTENTS

Phone Booth in Tujunga, CA / 1

Badlands / 3

Feral Kingdom / 4

Interstate / 6

The Bar Down The Street Where We Never Went / 7

The Radius of Everything / 8

Spiders at Night / 10

Death of the Cool / 12

Kingdom of the Night / 13

Secret Butcher / 15

Breadcrumbs / 16

Hidden by the Smell of Flowers / 17

That Car You Love But Don't Trust / 19

The Future You See In Her Eyes / 21

You Never Hear the Shot That Kills You / 22

The Ghost of Your Heart to Greet Me / 24

Breakwater Morning / 26

The Mice Have Abandoned the Woodpile / 27

Three White Pills / 29

Legs and Heels / 31

Not Unlike Feathers / 33

This Bird is on Fire / 35

Road Kill / 36

When We Talk About Dreams / 40

Death Row Escape / 42

No Harvest / 43

Apartment 5-D / 45

Cursed Ship / 47

My Ex's Father / 48

Peripheral Magic / 51

Blue Infinity / 53

Sunday May / 54

Strawberry Brunette / 55

The Postcard / 59

The Lost Rivers of Night / 60

New Streets, Old Streets / 61

Bright Skies, Cool Nights / 64

West Texas Skyway / 66

Where we're from the birds sing a pretty song, and there's always music in the air.

— The Man from Another Place

Phone Booth in Tujunga, CA

yellow gold hills of dust where that diner
tucked in among the pines and stone

it's where we had long talks of ex-
husbands and wives
over hamburgers and cokes spiked

with your flask of Jameson
before we headed back
out the door, but you left your smokes

inside and had to hit the ladies one last time
so I took the moment to use the old

phone booth by the road, door whining
open and fishing quarters from my

pocket to call back east, could still
hear *Old Shoes (and Picture Postcards)*

from your open car window, and all
of the sudden I didn't have anyone

to call, no number coming to mind so
important that I had to slide them quarters

home, so I didn't, I just waited for you
to come back to the car and we held hands

going faster and faster down those hills back
to the valley where we'd part ways at the

East Hollywood bus station later that night
knowing it was a long shot we'd ever

see each other again, but knowing the road
held stranger things than a reunion

so who knew? not us, not the fry cook, not Tom
Waits, or even the bus driver stealing me north

one last time along our golden coast
before we both became memories at last

Badlands

The back roads leading out of town wound across untilled farm fields in too-early spring with gray skies and rusted tractors, wayward barns red and tilted, the road dipping to cross small creeks and dry river beds, not quite New England, not quite Adirondack, and sometimes it was Springsteen or Petty or Neil Young murmuring through the car speakers in the deep background while silence choked the worldview—the mind toiling over how the pieces that made us one no longer fit, the answers so hard to come by, how talking wasn't helping, how loving wasn't loving anymore. Wide maples with ropes hanging where tire swings once twisted in the breeze lined the small roads out of town, roads damp with morning dew, so early still, with the feeling of how love doesn't last as long as the idea of love still visible in the air like a fog the sun couldn't burn away through overcast skies. Springsteen and the abandoned farm stand, the Hudson River and the ancient fields where men and women died in 1776, 1777, where crows jostle and stare as the road leads further and further away from morning church bells and small rooms and whispered conversations, frightened reactions, trembling lips, mistakes, all the goddamn mistakes, the innocent evils of our too-young marriage. The road goes on and on over the hills. It never started with our hands holding each other tight in December nights and it wouldn't end with our hands closing doors, turning keys, lifting last boxes into back seats either, would not end with waving goodbye. There is love and there is heartache. There is the road. None of it ends, even when it does. Hold on to that. Just keep holding on.

Feral Kingdom

a life lived out of boxes is a feral kingdom,
months and years in spaces borrowed,
couches loaned, small corners to call your own
so long as grace and luck and favors
hold out, but favors always fade
like streetlights at dawn
leaving nothing
but a vast sea of gray and hollow hearts

those dinner parties you once threw
back in your married twenties are
history book memories now,
daydreams of the transient sitting on
a bus bench staring into the middle nothing
with empty pockets

it's easy to feel like a failure,
working two jobs and still not
making enough to hold off
the legal bills, medical bills,
and also make rent, utilities,
keep gas in the car—daily
negotiations with intangibles
and inchoate hopes of
tomorrow and tomorrow
and every morning a sorrow
with another life to solve

yet you believe that maybe the next
for rent sign will be the one that really says *home*
and maybe the next piece
of mail that chases you down will
say *current balance $00.00*
and maybe the gods will whisper, *you've
seen enough, rest now, close your eyes and breathe*

because even if it's just enough room to stretch
your legs as they shovel dirt on top of you
and pray over books you've never read
with all those *amens* and with a *blessed be you*
that last home-sweet-home is still better
than never getting to unpack all those boxes
filled with what you were, what you'll never be
six feet deep and dreaming, same as it ever was

Interstate

when I woke the passenger
beside me had disappeared
departed somewhere along the way
maybe Kingston, maybe New Paltz
but their duffle bag was still
overhead, straps dangling down
swaying with the roll of the bus
along the nighttime highway
in the headlights of passing cars
I saw it was snowing now
but nothing was building up
on the shoulder of the highway
too warm, too damp, too late
and when we arrived in Albany
and all the ghosts of its streetlights
crowded the sidewalk to greet me
I left the bag there in the overhead
rack, understanding that we all
have our own journeys to make
and that finesse has little to do
with anything, whereas fate will
drag you down or light the way
to home or hell or both, but
only if you let it

The Bar Down The Street Where We Never Went

There was a bar around the corner and down the street, set back in the trees at the edge of the village. It was a dilapidated townie bar and only one of three within close driving distance, but I never went. Never went to any of them, in fact. It was that two-year period where I didn't drink because she didn't drink and we were going to do this together and even though I couldn't find work she didn't care and I'd send resumes and clean and cook and wait on the front stoop in the fading October light and watch for her car to turn the corner so we could begin; a kiss, a meal, and plan the next, and the next, and the weekend after. Those weekends were a diminishing wonderment, their stock falling, the supplies fading from life's pantry, but neither of us knew that yet. That townie bar back where the sidewalk ended at the treeline beyond crooked wooden houses was on my mind more and more on those front porch evenings, as the golden hue of the falling sun gave way to bruised night and cold winds. December lights, hands held to stay warm as we walked through the town's small parks, Christmas trees, closed antique shops, lit-up homes, townie bars full and bustling, slipping into bed quiet and solitary together, then one day solitary alone, in beds and in rooms far from that village and the little bar there within the woods, just around the corner and down the street where we never went, not once, not even after it all went down, down, down.

The Radius of Everything

there is little else to do but walk
down the street and study
the radius of sundry rain puddles

clear now, late morning
dampness in the air

up the walk and there
she is
notebook in hand

she drinks sherry in
white wicker chairs
flecked with rain

puddles ripple in the
autumn breeze

hell is pretending this isn't
a slow death

both of us pretending
pulling away in the crash of silence
and knowing for days,
absolute masters of this
remote mantra

she sits
two feet away
jotting notes to or about
someone as stray
beads of rain
peck at the sidewalk
below us

we haven't said a word in hours

and the leaves scurry sideways
all the time now

Spiders at Night

a bowl of pears and a stack
of 45 records in reflective vinyl
on the kitchen counter,
domestic signifiers, two pens,
a Joy of Cooking book leaning
against a bread box your dead
grandmother gave you ten years ago,
years and months and days of bread

you smashed a spider on the wall
with the heel of your fist;
outside in the November night a shadow
walks by with a dog casting
figures across the asphalt, shroud
over the moon, stillness, somnolence
a feeling you should call your father

at some point life slowed down and
sped up at the same time at the same
crossroads where all things are now
possible and none of them happen
and the pain comes in incremental
doses crawling higher and higher
through the orange bottles lining up
on your dresser, the minutes

spidering along, the years
counted one by one like the sound of
18-wheelers on the highway
on the other side of the fence
in the back yard nighttime desolation

I want to reach through time and space
and tell you one good thing after
another but we're at that crossroads
instead, where the words form but
nobody speaks, and the shadows move
in and out of streetlights, growing
shorter then longer, then gone

and I know what to say to you
I know how to express love, but
when I reach for the phone by the bowl
of pears, I pause and watch the highway
lights outside the window, in the cold
November nighttime and wonder who
how when where and sometimes why

Death of the Cool

sewing through Alamo Heights
after midnight, headlights and red lights
and Chet Baker, Miles, news of
your suicide in that cracked little
bungalow further downtown, soft
highway sounds like the ocean
we loved so well

your records and books were gone
by the time we got there to pay respects
but that's alright, we'll always
have the night, and all the
pain in the world

Kingdom of the Night

the best enemies we have
are the ones we love

they know the pathways
to the tomb

they know the combinations
and the warning lights

sometimes there is a deep swell
in the river at night

pulling from far downstream, shifting,
soon gone, replaced, and gone again

we cross this river each night,
but some day we won't

I can hear the heartbeat
of the world when the lights go out

I can hear the whisper of every
held moment you keep

and then the night you gave them away,
one after the other, lip to someone else's ear

black tide glass scattered across stone,
whiskey and macadam, a kingdom in the night

and when the wind dies and the swell recedes
we will walk this tomb together

forever in our secret hell
I will see to it

Secret Butcher

Outside the locust hum tunes the engine, greases the wheels, signals the brakeman, adjusts the halogen moon just enough to allow me to read these letters I write her on all the butcher's paper I have kept over the journey. The meat of my liver and heart and indelicate intangibles smear red and waxy behind the black ink taken from black skies, black memories of the knives she kept, the sharp ones, the dull ones, serrated and hooked, the narrow rapier-like final plunge that ended it with a smile and a kiss and a promise this long train would take me home. But I've been sitting here in the dark on this lost buffer stop. I see an abandoned outpost beyond, alkali pools of no water whiteness reflecting in the sun and the moon, a scythe of white hovering above the dead treeline, where all these letters catch in the wind, one by one, slipped out the window each time I finish one and begin the next. They are letters of love and remorse and promises of revenge to my secret butcher somewhere far behind me—and, I am sure, somewhere far ahead. The moon wanes toward me, lighting my way. I reach my hand for another scrap of glossy white, and begin again.

Breadcrumbs

at the edge of a highway
outside Little Rock
you may find the small pile
of half burned polaroids
depicting things we were
and no longer are
breadcrumbs
eaten by time
leaving us lost and sleepless
beneath railroad bridges
staring up at stars that were never
within reach
and are now burning out
one by one
broken bulbs gone, gone
leaving all of us little dust motes
of the universe trembling in the dark
at the edge of a highway
maybe outside Little Rock
maybe who knows where
anywhere, nowhere
lost in the feral kingdom of night

Hidden by the Smell of Flowers

4 a.m. and the water drips down
from the long ripples in the ceiling,
things like unhealed scars

the water collecting in the bucket
reeks of vomit and rot, of ancient
pipes and molding sheetrock

it has soaked into the mattress
where we used to sleep and sometimes
try to talk about why it wasn't
as good as it used to be

we didn't know it at the time, but
the stench of rot and vomit
was in the air there as well

hidden by the smell of flowers in
the vase on the nightstand, and by the
night air vibrating through the window
with the sound of car doors closing
and of highways, crickets, prayers

at all hours of the night, our life
and now it is 4 a.m. again
it has always been 4 a.m. again
the air is cool and the stink
is still here
while you are not

tap—tap goes the water
in the bucket as the streetlights
hum in dawn's coming light

you were right, we were wrong
and the water keeps falling

That Car You Love But Don't Trust

all four tires deflate overnight
so any time you leave you
have to stop at the gas station
down the hill and refill them, and probably
once more if you're out for too long,
not to mention the nail in the rear right
tire from driving through that construction
zone looking for orange traffic cones to steal
like an idiot

when she told you she loved you
you were unemployed;
the 85 Honda hatchback was leaking
gasoline and had a sock tied
to the bracket for the missing
windshield wiper, plus the four tires

you were both 21 and she told
you that she loved you

nobody told you they loved
you when you drove the 69 Mustang
or when you drove the Saab
with leather heated seats, it was always
in the one car you didn't trust

they wanted to make out for hours
and crawl into the back seat, and tell you
that they loved you
afterward

but this one was different
she went to a good
college, had a welcoming family,
and she loved that car and how awful
it looked going down the road
like life was going to explode any
minute, and she even filled the tank
every time you picked her up

four apartments later
three jobs later
two graduations later
one diamond ring later
and you're both
driving brand new Nissans
when you find she has been fucking
some guy from college
who still drove his father's BMW
a white one with heated leather seats

blowing your theory about bad cars and good love
all to hell
and probably blowing
more than that too, but you
don't like to think
about that, if you can help it

The Future You See In Her Eyes

when she turns up Tom Petty on the radio
late at night, taking the turns fast and wide
through foothills in Vermont straight through
to Saratoga Springs, singing "Refugee" and
"Here Comes My Girl" with the summer wind
whipping her hair into my face as I lean in
and smell destiny in the crook of her neck,
holding tight to this dark void of infinite joy
until the gas station comes into sight and she pulls in,
wanting soda and cigarettes, the mosquitoes
swarming the orange halogen parking lot lights
inside it's cool, our sweat chilling as we
decide on ice cream instead before heading back out
onto the open road, a straight shot into town now
for neon cocktails and pool hall laughter,
but there are miles of darkness yet and Tom singing
"You Got Lucky" with her hand in my hair,
making this feel like forever, even if it ended
too long ago to say it ever really happened;
we can't start believing it didn't, not yet, not us,
not until the summers end for good
and the music fades to nuclear
midnight radio static black white gone

You Never Hear the Shot That Kills You

there is no one right way to do it
but there are many wrong ways

most days are wrong, most nights
tedious with little moments of passing luck

and outside the window, bullets walk by
ripping into the cat's dream

the cat raising her head, yawning
and then slipping back to death

as the bullets walk by in their heels,
outside the window, searching

some men can't do it, can't take
all those artillery shells and BBs,

those .22s and .45s
can't shrug them off

they either kill on impact
or lodge themselves deep within

waiting, building up, strangling
the heartbeat, the lungs, the brain,

the spirit hiding inside the liver,
we feel each one, and you can see it

every time a bullet finds its mark
the white of the eyes turning infinite

for just one moment while the cats sleep
and you step forward, open a door

step into the night to
join the hail of gunfire

hoping, the dangling carrot of hope,
as the last bullet finds the heart at last

The Ghost of Your Heart to Greet Me

I don't understand where they went
the sparkling nerves
the delicate tendencies
or even just the ability to speak

I often wake in the night and see ghosts
walking in and around my open closet
and I feel nothing at all, I just stare
with no emotion and wonder which of the women
I have loved has died this time, or is it me now?
Is it my time? I see her, the first one,
roaming the halls sometimes, transparent
at 3 a.m., and I wonder if it is just the wisps
of passing headlights outside on Route 15 or if my
hallucinations have seeped into the nights
as they have mottled my days,
startling moments
where shrubs become dogs for an instant,
where insects jump across my skin, where shadows
leap and hew at my quiet afternoons
frightening moments of terror

that must be it, the ghosts are not
here tonight, and they are not
hallucinations, I simply wish

I would wake to something more significant
than the quiet hum of the air conditioner,
than the twisted sheets around my legs,
than the glass of water waiting on the bedside
table beside piles of books and my glasses

you see, I have removed my heart
and kept it in a jar in the bottom of my closet
for so long now that I am imagining
ghosts hunting for it, trying to twist it open and
bring it back to me

I wish they could
I can't take not sleeping anymore
and it is worse when I am not alone
mainly because it isn't her
her ghost, her heart, or even *her* memory
to greet me when I wake

Breakwater Morning

White embering spark of hope, you moon there, weaving the night loom yonder, you reflection of light and a lifetime walking through the night toward dawn, I can smell the long week on you, in your clothing and hair, staring up, a silhouette watching stars, connecting lifelines, tying nights and horizons with forever, or at least the images of forever that you harvest from the details we've nurtured, endless pieces of time, your eyes illuminated by somnolent jazz from somewhere nearby in the breakwater morning, music of water and rocks by the shore, the air fresh as the springtime hush of rain, and here comes the tide again, morning light glinting and a smile like the dew cast over wildflower fields behind us for miles and miles and it's so far now that we can never go back, though sometimes I like to think we can, just keep walking out into the breakwater embrace until it takes hold, swallows, assimilates every cell and memory—but we're not quite ready for that, hand in mine, hand in yours, not quite yet indeed.

The Mice Have Abandoned the Woodpile

it's so cold that you sweat,
shivering and alone in a small room
as the phone lights up with
digital daggers and questions of whether
you're seeing someone new
and wouldn't it be nice to catch
up over drinks at one of the old places?

outside, the wind across the lake makes the
cold worse than it really is, and it's bad enough
that the mice have abandoned the woodpile
to hide in the walls inside here where
they still freeze to death,
and you'll know where come spring

it is three days to New Year's Eve and she
already has her plans and won't you be a
part of them? early afternoon cocktails? but
you think by not replying you're winning,
except you both know it hurts, you both
know the streets are snowing themselves in,
that time piles up higher and higher to end
all things, all inroads, all escape routes

it's so cold you sweat as you wonder
what to say to her or anyone anymore, spying
through the curtain at the chopping maul, the pile
of wood waiting, the frozen lake beyond,
and the phone buzzing brings you back,
always brings you back, lighting up your face
in the blue silence of the small room

what will you do? what will you do?
now and forever
decide

Three White Pills

dust begins to pile up
faster than you think

three months in this
new place and there it is

sheeting the coffee table
and the bookshelves

including the one where the three
white pills sit among the Steinbecks
and the Vonneguts

its my medicine shelf
and I am low on the painkillers
but I have plenty of Steinbeck
and there's McCullers in
there too, the medical texts
that keep me alive and honest

below are all the empty orange
pill bottles, emptied out like bones
without marrow, like my
heart in the 11 p.m. lamplight
surviving on fumes

on images of faceless people
who I once loved and once loved me

and now I have three white pills
just enough to dull the pain of this

not enough to make this go away

like pulling a sheet over the face
of the dead

three white pills

swallow, swallow, swallow

turn out the light
try to remembers the prayers
your mother taught you
as a child, but too much time
has passed, and the words never come
so I pull the sheet over my face
and wait

Legs and Heels

simmering predawn
in summertime
disarray,
black stilettos wound
in black stockings on
the floor, knotted notions
holding us against the sheets,
tidal thoughts of hands, red
marks across our shoulders
and her soft morning breath
unconscious, relieved

birthmark on her calf in the morning sun
sensation of time returning
nectarous dignities
rising from the fugue

now there's visceral consciousness
where our names exist
legs and heels
appear from beneath white
sheets like animals
cresting from a strange foreign sea

small lines of purple
bruises, bitemarks

along collarbones
and necks

on her wall is a clock with a dead
battery inside and hands that
point to six and seven and I remember
how I used to love her but we
ruined everything, then fought a war
to win back a city, a street, a small
room where we could hold out
for one last night, then rise
and catch sight of each other as
we dress and wonder
which of us became the prisoner
and which of us would break
for the treeline first

Not Unlike Feathers

yellow walls peeling / revealing
white and blue and the tone of human
flesh / a pale peach sort of death
from generations ago when
ghosts lived in this space and used
horses / gas lamps / hand-rolled
wax candles / knives against
chickens living in small sheds
where we now leave our old
christmas trees to rot

but they don't rot
they only grow hard and sharp
like all things

if you pull up the carpet you'll
find hardwood / beneath
and under
the pale peach sort of flesh
you'll find bones molting to
gray flakes not unlike feathers that
may yet take to the air / who's to
say what they'll do when
I am gone

there's always more to find
the deeper you go
and you may not see it
and you may not know it
but it's there / the very tendrils
of stardust machinations
settling between and beneath
every universal element / beyond
blood and lava
the plasma infinite unseen
hot steam rising from a mug
of earl gray tea before dawn

simple things that are shapeless
and without texture / for now

give it time / eventually
someone will drag all these things
out back and let them harden
in the cold winter sun
and then we will see the truth

This Bird is on Fire

No southern stars in the orange glow night. Here in this city, airplanes like birds on fire cross in slow motion, dilated nights, highways snaking through veins shaking through nerves rattling through bones and my bloodline is there on the couch, lying still when I arrive at 2 a.m. from endless drinking every night, drinking to forget, and my bloodline is dead there, not dead but almost dead, dying, stroking out two or three times a year, breathing deep, slow, my father on his couch at 2 a.m., and I want to cry for him and everything he never got to be but I can't cry, I don't cry, I haven't been able to cry since signing the divorce papers and swallowing the pills, the ones doctors gave me, the ones women in bars gave me, the ones friends in parked cars at night gave me in small paper bags, watching them drive away as I swallowed pill, pill, pill, stare up at the night sky of this boiling city and watch the airplanes like birds on fire, red and white, crossing the sky of midnight neon orange, taking the highways, snakes in a pit, opening my father's door, all of us dying, nobody crying, breathing, lights out, the end.

Road Kill

the zipper woke me and I saw the last of her
leg going through the tent flap,
then I turned back to sleep

small voices and the crackling of autumn
fire with bacon, coffee, bitter remains
of a cold night and dead love

Adirondack ground zero for our
three-year old marriage, 7:13 a.m.

dressed in double flannel, the top layer
belonging to her father, I stepped
out into the bright morning and kept
walking past greetings and knowing eyes

I headed for the road beyond the trees

getting out of the campsite felt better
getting away from crowded
humanity packing in among towering
pines to play primitive
for a weekend, it made me sick
and it made me sick
to have my illness thrown at my face, my distaste

for plastic humanity becoming a knife
in whispered accusations at night

her eyes narrowed every time she knew
I wanted to recede from
everything and everyone, had to,
dour, couldn't just let people
enjoy themselves, it's like being married to Eeyore
she said, which made me laugh

she capped the evening with:
you're driving me away

same as it ever was

the road was a long way through the trees
and I couldn't hear any voices
only the sound of shoes on dead needles
and twigs and forgiving soil

the ground rose to a wooden guardrail
and I sat on the prone telephone pole,
the autumn pavement scattered with leaves
and far to the right, a small pile of swollen
organs and fur, no flies, no movement
death waiting on macadam

I remembered the words *an iron will
is often prey to magnetism*

but I always thought of magnetism in reverse
the repellency of stubbornness
or maybe ignorance, the inability to change
the inability to see

driving her away, the act of driving
the active form of the noun drive
>   *1. a trip or journey in a car*
>   *2. an innate, biologically-determined*
> *urge to attain a goal or satisfy a need*

an iron will
running headlong
through the forest of pines
toward the wooden
guardrail, and I feel that old
danger forming inside
the urge for too much whiskey
the urge to drink myself
into a blackout state so none
of this could touch me anymore

rising from the guardrail, I heard the sound
of the logging truck
taking the curve so fast in
the autumn Adirondack morning
and I knew there was
more than one way to find

that dark comforting state of stasis

stepping into the autumn
pavement

testing my iron will
and magnetism

When We Talk About Dreams

movement or the impossibility
of movement, that
is what makes our dreams stay
with us
through horrible
decades and silent years
trapped in the back seat of mom's
yellow station wagon, unable
to move, yet the car races onward
crashing headlong into
cars, trees, finally the guardrail
over the edge of the bridge

a dream,
movement or the impossibility

the dream is one where I am
unable to move, unable to escape
yet whatever we fear moves
with such ease
it comes and you know it comes
and you cannot move for all
your struggling and fury
and awareness
for all your ascension and
wisdom and karma

we always fight
we always fight that which
comes for us, taking
all forms and incarnations
the beautiful and the
scarred, the holy and the
slithering evil of ignorance
all moving toward us with speed, hoping
to pull us deeper, pin us down
for good, sink in its teeth

I am no longer talking about dreams

I never was, and neither were you

Death Row Escape

hotel rooms and the endless waiting
at windows holding waterfalls of orange
curtains in one clutched hand

the phone beside the bed stares, the bath
runs, mistakes hang
from the ceiling like a thousand
idling hangman ropes

these hotel rooms and days of waiting
grind bone-on-bone
every check-in an arraignment
every check-out a parole
a part of you never leaves my sight
a part of you always waits below my barred windows
and the water begins to flow
over the edge of the tub, which lets
the curtain fall, which makes
the phone ring, and there
you are
another life sentence pardoned

and now the coat,
the tie and the fedora,
the key in the lock

a thousand crimes of the heart imagined
a criminal on the loose once more

No Harvest

the rotting of apples
and the memory stains
they leave behind
tall tufts
of Mohawk grass, odd
discoloration

the stray apples dribble along autumn
walkways and sunsets and empty

ladders leading up to the thin
weak branches, bereft of any fruit

across the dirt road the lopsided pumpkins
grow fat off the sun and prickly green vines

flies drift as the wind crawls,
the smell of honey
and mowed grass bringing on the night

the forced return to bad love and having
to deal with bad love face to face

no more apple pie nights
in front of a movie
no more ice cream whispers, no weekends

of rest, and no apples to pick
because the ladders are all broken

and now the flies die as the night wind crawls,
the scent of new honey in new fields

and when the morning staggers along the dirt road
maybe this will all be like a bad dream

a hallucinatory Halloween, a fresh dawn
revealing the apple trees glowing
with dew, maybe with
one ladder
leaning crooked, waiting
in the tall cool grass

maybe, keep saying maybe

Apartment 5-D

there is a square of cement on her street
where one can stand and see
her shadow moving across her ceiling

a shadow of our history, and as comforting
as the image of her face burned into
night-vision may be, why
swim to the bottom of that pool and
slowly release tiny bubbles
of oxygen until it all goes dark?
mistake her scent for oxygen?
better to avoid the very state, much less
the city, block, building with
her name on the mailbox, her initials on
a sticker by the buzzer,
her footsteps on the floor somewhere beyond,
her hair across a pillow as
sheets crease the soft skin of her cheek,
shoulder, chest, forearms

someone once tried
to explain to me I should
build a new life from the ground up in some
crossroads of a village that never heard
a name like hers, never saw shades of hazel
and brown eyes quite like hers,

a town with two traffic lights,
two gas stations, an ice cream parlor that closes
at eight, where the street lights switch
off and on all night long, a Morse-code message
begging the past to stay away
if only for one more night

they tried to explain, they tried
but the city calls, and the lights beckon
and I roam the filth and the steel
like a ghost, content with shadows and
her name, a number, a letter
that's all

Cursed Ship

derelict ships in the moonlight howling
chances at us through the riptide, chances
scuttled by fire, by what lies deep below,
long tentacles of self-abuse curling up
to meet thrashing legs and reaching arms,
those derelict ships with ruined hulls
rising free of the ocean floor, drifting
away from the dead coastal city with no
lights, no love, only memories
that come to you in the night when
you're treading water to remind you
how you screwed it all up, the things
you said and did, the chances you missed,
the chances you missed, the chances
drifting away in the night, the rictus moon
bearing witness to your head slipping
down, into the black, the deep, the rest
of your days and nights as derelict jetsam
as you think about what you've done
and down, down, down you go again

My Ex's Father

casually monolithic in a Stones t-shirt
smoking on the back patio
in the haze of infinite Sunday

he never asked me what I saw in his daughter
he never asked me to treat her right
or get her home early, just tossed me his
keys and let me move in when she
was away at college and I was homeless,
talked humanist indulgence and
vinyl records, Long Island
summers, and when Zeppelin jumped
the shark or if they ever did

he bought weed off my friends
but voted Republican and traveled
with Phish and would ask me
to drive him to the supermarket
sipping a Corona in the passenger seat,
a smoke dangling from his
lips and he'd go inside and come
back with lotto tickets and a sixer while
never having put on shoes that day

I'd lay in my girlfriend's bed and
when she'd come home her head would

fit right in the crook of my neck and
we'd plan out a dream house,
double-headed showers,
woodstove, a library with one of
those ladders with wheels that rolled along
the walls lined with books, and we wanted
a guest cottage for her old man
so he'd always be around, and that made
us both really happy, we'd just shut
up and stare at the ceiling, smiling

she loved him but I idolized him, and
I think the difference was she wanted
someone like him to always be in her life
and I wanted to be what he was so effortlessly
but I knew I'd never get there, it was out
of reach for someone so *shiftless when idle*
as Paul Westerberg would scream when I played my
car radio too loud fixing the taillights

with him sitting on a stack of old tires riding
my ass about my shit garage band music and
laughing, seeing me get defensive, making
me laugh too, and god damn I missed
him when it had to end, hated leaving him
behind almost as much as leaving her
but she had fucked just a few too many guys
out there in Chicago and so I had to
pack my shit car up and find somewhere

else to be until the next one came
when I saw his obituary a decade later
I almost reached out, but the obit
was two years old online and there
wasn't anything else to tell her anyway
so I just drove to the supermarket without
shoes and bought a sixer of Corona
and drove to the river that night
playing early Zeppelin before
hucking the empties into the Hudson
River and hoping they made their
way to Long Island somehow,
little empty messages in bottles
sending my thanks homeward bound

Peripheral Magic

the trash cans here
do not reflect the sun

it is quiet

you know when you're in love
and you see
the world through
his or her eyes? through
the eyes of this person
you love?

you see films
differently or hear
a song differently or notice
how your hometown is so
very quiet
to the point of discomfort

you see a dog walking
down the street
with a dead bird in its jaws

you wonder if this is symbolic,
if any of the small peripheral
events that make a morning have

anything in common,
if they connect like ethereal
spiderweb threads with
morning dew
diamonding across
their strands

don't be foolish
there is no peripheral magic
in dead birds
in dead garbage cans
in a sun that burns
whether or not your god exists

or even love, which is a wonderful
magic trick
a diversionary illusion of awe
and emotion
and when the rabbit is pulled
from the hat you see it is real,
you throw up your hands and
say it's you and me and look
how everything is new again,
look how we see with eyes so fresh

while the dead bird
hangs
from the jaws of a black dog
in the morning sun
burning with all its might

Blue Infinity

that evening with you
standing shoulder to shoulder at
the window overlooking
Main Street
where music and crowds
and children carrying sparklers
run silver cascades of shadow and fire
over you leaning into me
at the dawn of a new era now gone

now this coffin town is lined with red silk,
mahogany, silence
and I look up from the bottom
of the grave and see that window
and the shadows of who we were

two clouds undone by time
and cast into the blue
that rises forever
into infinite highway black

Sunday May

I can't tell you that I saw your father's grave last Sunday, or that I walked past the house where you grew up, where we fell in love. What I can say is that even ships that sink to the bottom of the sea might be found again; not recovered, but not lost to time. A footnote in history that cannot live but cannot really die. And while your own grave doesn't listen now the way I didn't listen then, I'll keep diving into the dark as penitence, bringing light to the deep for as long as I can, until I join you all in the forever sway of this black tide embrace.

Strawberry Brunette

Smitty's Pub had failed us often
with rancorous invitations in neon,
filthy floors and crooked pool cues,
bent darts, the smell of whiskey,
beer rings on rickety wooden tables,
   let it be so
and we were holding steady on a Friday night,
long after midnight when I went to go
pick a song on the jukebox
   and a strawberry brunette
approached and said my friend
at the bar told her I was a writer, and
   so was she (there's always one
somewhere)

and this is how it begins, sayeth the lord,
reciprocal dogmas and poetry,
and soon consecrations
and tasting rum
in her mouth, and can I
tell her how
it all works, how
to actually get published

of course

she wants to write horror, but not
that erotica horror shit, she says, the stuff
you see on bookshelves in Walmart,
no, no, rather the real horror—she wants to write
stories about meeting men in bars
and taking them home and murdering them
while they slept after fucking
   I nod along, looking for my friend over
her shoulder, and he appears with the strawberry
brunette's roommate, a surly dishwater blonde
who begins telling me I'm an asshole
for trying to pretend I'm a writer
   just to get laid

it's a sanctuary argument of sorts, gets us
away from talk about murder
and the strawberry brunette tells her
to shut the fuck up, turns and asks
me if I like her hair, she dyed
it red herself, kind of goth but not like
you know high school goth, you know?

it's strawberry brunette, I tell her,
but she isn't listening

we all talk a bit about whether to stay
or go, and they decide to go
find another bar, maybe someplace
   darker, you know?

the strawberry brunette asks
if she can drive my car as we walk outside
and I tell her no, so she takes
my hand with the key ring slid up
my finger and puts my finger
in her mouth, slowly tries to pull
the keys off my finger with her teeth but
it's awkward and funny and we laugh
and she says if I let
her drive she won't slit my throat
when we're lying in her bed afterward

my friend and the dishwater blonde
are having a similar sort of argument over
by his car and I steer us that way
   where we banter hysterical laughter
back and forth
   kind of floating through the night
making out in the dark
   of the parking lot and she again whispers in
my ear how she still wants
to drive my car, but the dishwater
has lost all of her patience,
is walking toward her truck calling,
C'mon, screw these guys,
I'm bored

the strawberry brunette laughs and says
it's my last chance but I've already
fallen on the side of not wanting to die

just to get inside something crazy on a Friday
   so I back away, put an arm on my friend's
shoulder as they climb into a tan truck

   he says we should go after them
and as they slowly drive our way he
   walks toward them, waving as they blow
kisses from the window, and he runs
and leaps in the bed of the truck as they
pass, except they don't seem to notice

and they turn the corner out of the lot
and they're gone

a half-hearted panic rushes over me
and I think about getting
in my car to follow,
   but I don't, I sit on the hood
and smoke from a shitty Camel
pack I stole from someone
inside the bar and wait for
a phone call from him
my cell in hand
a feeling of hunger
a desire to go back in the bar
to wait for the fates to show me which
way to go, home or after him wherever he ended up,
waiting on the fates, because they haven't
steered me wrong yet,
   still being alive as I was

The Postcard

There is a postcard of a painting of a cemetery from the eighteenth century on my refrigerator door and outside there's a metal road sign for the hospital where children are born and sometimes die, and in between are homes like mine, silent and dark at 11:21 pm, and I am staring at this postcard and thinking of pain and mistakes and my mother and father out there, of people I love but never speak to, and we are all so still and quiet, crooked on the wall of the fridge, held by weak magnets and fate, our tombstones pale in the eighteenth century moonlight, a small reminder that if I wake and rise tomorrow, I should try harder, love better, and make it clear and true and real—but one thing at a time, there's still a whole night to somehow get through first.

The Lost Rivers of Night

in the crawling hours
after your call your blue shadow
skims easy across the black canvas of the hotel wall,
and for a little while it's like
you're there, aching thoughts
calming to soft whispers
the motes of your laughter floating
above in the lilting moonlight

there are things your voice will do to me
that no pill can accomplish,
and this feeling makes the moon feel familiar,
brings it near, filling the bedroom with
infinity white

other times, the night weights down
hellish and suffocating
with the once dormant history of what we were,
but those nights when your voice arrives,
it is a small reprieve, a brief return, the horror
of humanity drifting away
as sleep takes me down to the lost rivers of night
where everything outruns the end, the last
dial tone we'll ever hear before
the sea greets us with arms so wide
we'll never see another safe place
ever again

New Streets, Old Streets

try to catch every drop
try everything
  be the recorder
  be the rolling
wheel wrapping tight
taking in every moment
  correctly

massive ignorance and desks in a row
paperwork and time sheets
homework and SATs
  so many lives
dying with each dawn
up and ready and out
  knowing nothing about
themselves or the
sun

I miss the one kiss
that will bring the downpour,
the reign of the speedy past
  and so I step back into the night
  and look skyward
embrace nobody but myself
my own fearful
  self

bad dreams
bad Karma
bad love wandering down
  new streets
  old streets
it makes no difference
when all you do is
run
from one hell to the next

the raincoat evening and the journey
onward, like a corkscrew
  the holy corkscrew
  the waiting bottle
broken by summer, by fall,
by winter, shards like the knife she
held in her hand
that you had to take away, telling
her it would be okay
when you knew otherwise

those leftover emotions
  those pitfalls inside
  they send you reeling while waiting
at the bus stop
  joining the beggars
  bleeding as one
turning upward to the falling

   luck of destruction and time
you record it all, all you
can

why?
  don't ask why

run

Bright Skies, Cool Nights

I witness love every day
the entwined heartstrings of the young
like fleeting robins in blue June skies
I witness this in every passing face
as I sit, an old man on a bar stool,
or at least feeling like an old man, adrift in this world
where *home* is a word and nothing more

when you love someone you have
firm ground to land upon, a perch in a tree
and when you are alone you just fly
and fly, taking the gussets of wind
as well as you can, hoping to catch the next,
hoping to glide the years as long as possible
watching the seas churn below
watching for land, for rest, for shelter

and yet, search as we may,
we see love every day
we are not strangers to the feeling
we are not immune
you and I and all of us in this world
of bright skies and cool nights of
neon and cracked downtown asphalt
where the bars still call and the men

are tall and handsome, the women
with long hair and laughter like springtime
songs from sparrows and robins
or bright red tanagers in budding willow trees

this world is full of love and loneliness
and they reside side by side
it is beautiful and hurtful and
if this is the only home I'll know, this stool
in the eye of the summertime storm,
then I will sit tall, no matter the hour
or the years falling away
and I will glide as long as I can
searching, singing, until I too
fall into that deep blue sea that rolls
and rolls forever

West Texas Skyway

In the west there was a highway and my father drove us beneath the stars. My sister and I, the forever summertime, an endless void ahead. They were the kind of stars and skies unseen in the east, from the cities and suburbs and even the rural farm roads in upstate New York and Vermont. It was never so dark anywhere else in our lives as it was along that empty highway in western Texas with my father and sister. Town after town, no traffic lights. Hardly towns, hardly anything. A hotel we passed still had a stop on the local railroad line but had no parking lot aside from dirt. Stones turned white in the daytime and ran infinity black against the skies of night. Those skies, those stars, their lights palpable, their ghost echoes, ethereal blue and green in the shadows of mountains. Car headlights cut like razors against the black film of night, falling to the editor's floor, and my father is somewhere else now, my sister somewhere further, all of us tangled up down and low by circumstance and distance and medical financial emotional burdens. And if you take all this sky in as one, all these strips of black film lying cut and looping in the darkness of the universal projection room you'll see us still out there in the night, on that highway, deep within a feral kingdom beneath those stars, talking about observatories and motel pools and how much we love each other and no matter how old we get we'll always have that. We'll always have that, father. We'll always have that, sister. Endless stars of the universe so far above you've become one within me all this time.

James H. Duncan is the editor of *Hobo Camp Review* and the author of *Nights Without Rain, Dead City Jazz, What Lies In Wait,* and *We Are All Terminal But This Exit Is Mine,* among other collections of poetry and fiction. Between jobs at daily newspapers, overnight security posts, and magazines like *Writer's Digest,* he spends most of his time wandering train station platforms, quiet dive bars, and roadside diners looking for a hot meal, a good rest, and a little inspiration. He also reviews indie bookshops at his blog, *The Bookshop Hunter.* For more about his work, visit www.jameshduncan.com.

d-product-compliance